WILLPOWER 101

Dr. Talya Miron-Shatz and the Buddy&Soul team

INTRODUCTION: WELCOME TO WILLPOWER 101

You know what you want to do and where you want to go… You may have accomplished most of it, but you could use some extra oomph. Learn how you can strengthen your willpower by understanding the psychology behind it. You can increase your self-control, helping you stay motivated and on course so you can reach, maintain, and exceed your goals.

There are three goals that we had in mind while creating this book. We want you to:

- Understand the psychology behind willpower.

- Learn and apply practical tools to help you work towards greater self-control.

- Envision and plan your future successes, with the help of willpower

You're feeling determined and committed and you are *killing* that new diet, exercise routine, work and study schedule, and daily meditation practice. You're resisting temptations left, right, and center and feeling on top of the world.

Well, fast forward about a week and a half. You haven't made it to the gym, what with all the other to-dos on your list, but it's still in the plan. Maybe you'll double up on your workout tomorrow.
And then a month or two later, there is no longer any sign remaining of your resolution or its previous existence. No more gym. No new diet. No more feeling on top of the world.

Well, what exactly just happened?

You had a goal in mind, you figured out how you would fit it in your day; perhaps you even had all the right equipment. But, just like that, the momentum fizzled out.

That's where willpower comes in. Willpower is the unique force that you can harness within yourself to make your goals a reality. It is made up of a combination of self-control, motivation, and perseverance that helps you reach your goals.

Amazingly, willpower can be developed and strengthened, and that's where we come in. Even if it hasn't been one of your finer points in the past, join us as we explore the psychology behind this powerful characteristic. You'll learn valuable tools to keep you motivated to overcome laziness and procrastination so that you can flex your willpower muscles and feel what a difference it makes.

No matter what your goals in life, willpower is the energy that will help you stop procrastinating and resist temptation until you get to where you want to be.

So, let's go through this course together and learn more about the incredible mental muscle we all possess, called willpower.

YOUR JOURNEY TO WILLPOWER 101

HOW TO USE THIS BOOK TO FIND YOUR WILLPOWER

In this book you'll find ten great strategies for achieving the goals we listed above. You'll also find inspiring content and exercises you can engage with to help you practice willpower.

You will get the most out of this book by going through the strategies and associated exercises one by one. Of course, you can also simply read it the whole way through. But we recommend using this book by going through it in order, watching the TED talks, and doing the exercises. We have found the best way to do the exercises is by dedicating a notebook as your course journal. If you're reading this book on a PC, feel free to create a text file and use that as your course journal. Or you could simply use a good ol' pen and paper to do the exercises. Either way, we recommend keeping some method of writing handy while you go through the exercises in this book to optimize what you get out of it.

To maximize your experience with the Buddy and Soul book, share your thoughts and insights with us on social media! Post pictures relating to your progress on Instagram and Twitter, tagging @Buddy_N_Soul, and Facebook @Buddy&Soul. Direct message us YOUR story @Buddy_N_Soul on Instagram and be anonymously featured for a chance to **win a Buddy&Soul three month free membership**.   By sharing with us on social media, not only can you help others with their personal journeys, you can read about those facing similar challenges.

If you really want to go all the way, visit our website, BuddynSoul.com, and explore all that we have to offer beyond 'Willpower 101'. In fact, we have three other books in the wellness series that we think you might benefit from: Stress Management, Cultivating Authenticity, and Declutter Your Mind

I'm Dr. Talya Miron-Shatz, CEO of Buddy&Soul, where Willpower 101 and many more e-courses and books come from. I have a PhD in psychology and was very fortunate to do my post-doc at Princeton University with Nobel Laureate Daniel Kahneman. I've also taught at the Wharton Business School, University of Pennsylvania. Now I'm a professor at the Ono Academic College, and a visiting researcher at Cambridge University. I used to study happiness, and for a long time now, I've been studying medical decision making and helping organizations support people on their way to joy and health. One thing that struck me as unfair was that we were expecting people to change their life for good but weren't giving them the tools to do so. People deserve all the help they can get when breaking out of old patterns and moving their lives forward.

This is what Buddy&Soul does.

We support you in many ways by providing science-based actionable ways to sustain your body and mind. We help you sleep better, spark a change in your eating habits, and manage stress. We teach you how to create new habits and how to engage your willpower. We help you grow, claim your self-esteem, cultivate authenticity, reframe your life story, achieve your goals and so much more. Including Willpower 101.

We created unique course clusters for people dealing with specific challenges: students, patients, and pregnant women.

Everything you need to change your life for good.

I want to hear from YOU! Please feel free to send me an email with your thoughts, suggestions, and feedback regarding this book to talya@buddynsoul.com. I would love to hear what you think about this book and how it helped you with your willpower. Your feedback is extremely valuable and will allow us to help more individuals, like yourself, to obtain the necessary tools and support needed to change their lives for good.

I'm glad that you've decided to join us for the Willpower 101 course. Each session of our course consists of a warm-up talk followed by a hands-on component where you'll learn a new skill or idea and have a chance to start putting it into action.

We're going to start the Willpower 101 course by taking a look at what willpower is and what role it plays in our day-to-day lives.

In the talk we're about to watch, social psychologist Roy Baumeister speaks about self-control and willpower. He describes many benefits that people who exercise self-control experience and how we can increase our willpower. As you watch, think about the ways in which you'd like to strengthen your willpower.

We think you'll find that the more you put into the course, the more you'll get out of it. So, take full advantage of all our features and find your place in a community of people facing similar challenges.

Enjoy!

Watch 'Self-Control & Willpower' presented by Roy Baumeister on YouTube.

EXERCISE

Step 1: **Take this scientifically validated questionnaire to see where your current self-control and willpower stand.** Rate each statement from 1-5 **1** being a statement that describes you **very poorly**, and **5** a statement which is **very much like you**. Be as honest as possible for an accurate result.
(This scientifically validated questionnaire was built by Angela Duckworth, a leading academic, psychologist and author on grit and self-control).

1. New ideas and projects sometimes distract me from previous ones.
2. Setbacks don't discourage me.
3. I have been obsessed with a certain idea or project for a short time but later lost interest.
4. I am a hard worker.
5. I often set a goal but later choose to pursue a different one.
6. I have difficulty maintaining my focus on projects that take more than a few months to complete.
7. I finish whatever I begin.
8. I am diligent.

Your results:
4-5:
   You have a pretty solid self-control. Though staying motivated is hard, you manage to keep your goal in mind and practice willpower on a daily basis. This course will help you strengthen this power for a long-lasting effect in your future goals.
3:
   Your self-control is pretty good, but you are probably looking for a little more guidance in the area of willpower. Most times, you succeed in sticking to goals, and this course will solidify what you already know: that willpower will help you achieve your goals.
1-2:
   Your self-control needs a boost. You probably already know the ways in which poor willpower or self-control has affected your life. This course will help you create a lasting change and achieve goals in your life that you may previously have thought impossible.

Step 2: Based on what the questionnaire revealed, **write your impressions about your current willpower.** Were you surprised at what the test revealed? Disappointed? Motivated to start the course? Note your thoughts in your journal.

TIPS

Tip 1: If you scored low on your questionnaire, don't despair. Remember that your score is just a starting point, we are here to help increase your willpower.

Tip 2: The more honest you are with yourself the greater impact it will have on your success in the Willpower 101 course.

13 Fresh insights about willpower

Current research is painting willpower in a whole new light. Here are some evidence-based 'ahas' that can change the way you think about willpower.

1. The magic ingredient behind self-control is willpower.
2. Working on self-control helps improve one's self-esteem. You're more likely to succeed, in general, with more self-control.
3. According to scientific studies, people with self-control (i.e. who can exercise willpower) live longer.
4. Exercising willpower and self-control means having the capacity to change oneself.
5. By using your willpower muscle, you increase self-regulation.
6. We desire things all day, every day! Our willpower is *constantly* being challenged. That's why it's hard to control it.
7. Willpower is not a constant force. It fluctuates throughout the day depending on how much you have used it.
8. The more we use our willpower, the more depleted it becomes. And unless we 'recharge' it, we will be running on empty, which is a fancy way of saying standing still.
9. Resisting things depletes us of our willpower energy; better to avoid in order to keep our willpower strong.
10. The more you exercise your willpower, the stronger it becomes – in all areas.

Add your items to the list:

11. ____

12. ____

13. ____

13 Signs that your willpower needs boosting

How will you know if the time has come to boost your willpower? If any of these sound familiar, the time may be ripe.

1. Has your electricity and water been disconnected? Remember that pile of by your front door? Be sure that whoever sent them knows you are *planning* on paying them...
2. You've smoked that one last cig far more times than you can remember.
3. Mom is still waiting for you to return her call from last summer. And so is your kid's teacher. And so is your banker.
4. (Number of times you've said, "we should do something together, as a family") — (number of times you've actually done something together, as a family) = (number of times you've said, "we should do something together, as a family.")
5. Diet. Should we go into detail?
6. Even though it's been a long time since you last watched *Mary Poppins,* you still occasionally try snapping your fingers at the clutter, hoping that maybe this time it'll organize itself back into the cupboards.
7. You still have to use your GPS when driving to the gym.
8. You were only going to buy that nice shirt you needed for work, but there was a sale and... Oops.
9. Although very pretty, your 'to do' list was not intended as a decoration.
10. If your tomorrows would have known how many things you had planned for them, they would surely take a day off.

Add your items to the list:

11. ____

12. ____

13. ____

Why change my willpower? I'm happy with who I am!

If it ain't broke, don't fix it. I mean seriously, if I'm doing more-or-less okay with my current level of willpower, why bother with all this hard work?

For:

    1. There's always pressure to conform to the latest and greatest. Today it's willpower and tomorrow it'll be fur-lined, sequin-covered, leopard-print pants. I'd much rather just be my non-conforming self.

    2. Happiness with who I am is a much more valuable undertaking of my time than working on my willpower.

    3. I'm not going to fall into this trap! Willpower is something that you can't even change. It's like a bigger-boned person trying to shrink themselves to a size 0 – it's not going to happen. Better to accept myself for who I am.

    Add you own argument:

    4. ____

Against:

    1. I'm happy with myself now, but I know I'll just be that much happier after I work on my willpower.

    2. I don't let fear of the unknown make me shy away from life. Albeit scary, I know that working on my willpower and becoming more determined will only lead to bigger and better things.

    3. Better to change now when things in my life are working for me than wait until I fall into full-fledged crisis mode. Make a change when things are good. That's what I say!

    Add you own argument:

    4. ____

The moment I figured out what willpower means to me

Sometimes, all it takes is one incident, one experience, or even one fleeting moment to teach you the true value of willpower. Share your own experience – how did you learn what willpower meant to you? Spend five minutes writing about your experience with in your 'Willpower 101' journal.

Direct message us YOUR story @Buddy_N_Soul on Instagram and be anonymously featured for a chance to **win a Buddy&Soul three month free membership**.

STRATEGY 2: Learn to trust your willpower

Do you remember the beloved children's classic *The Little Engine that Could*? In this sweet story, a little blue train rescues another engine that has stalled and successfully pulls him up the hill with the determined chant of "I think I can."

It might sound oversimplified, but research shows that there's truth to the power of believing in your ability to persevere.

A study by Carol Dweck and colleagues demonstrated a strong connection between willpower and beliefs. They found that an individual's perspective about the availability of willpower may impact his or her ability to have self-control and complete tasks. In other words, the little blue train wasn't sure if she could successfully pull the other train, but she believed in her ability to try. that, in a nutshell, is willpower.

In his book *Self-Discipline*, Dominic Mann contends that in order to develop more willpower, you need to believe that willpower is a resource that can increase. While willpower can be depleted, which we'll talk more about later, it can also be regenerated. Recognizing that your basic abilities can be developed is called having a growth mindset.

If you believe the opposite, that willpower is limited and can't increase, you might actually get stuck in that. A 2010 study by Clarkson and colleagues showed that participants' perception of whether their willpower was depleted or not significantly affected their ability to perform, independent of their actual level of willpower depletion.

While it's astounding that beliefs and mindsets are so influential, it's encouraging too, because it means **you have the ability to affect your willpower.**

If you are taking this course to increase your willpower, I'd venture to assume that you do believe that willpower can grow, and that's an important starting point.

In fact, we are going to practice a visualization exercise where you will imagine what it would be like to have more willpower. Engaging your imagination is one way to build trust in the fact that your willpower can, in fact, grow.

Hi, and welcome! Let's continue deepening our understanding of willpower.

There is a lot of discussion today about the importance of encouraging children to use their imaginations. But what about us, the adults? Are there benefits to us using our imaginations?

According to high-performance business consultant, speaker, strategic illustrator and author Patti Dobrowolski, there are. You may be surprised to hear how we can leverage the power of imagination to actualize a vision of the future.

As you watch the talk, think about your own life. How can you leverage the power of your imagination to harness your willpower and tap into your inner strength?

Watch 'Draw Your Future' presented by Patti Dobrowolski at TEDxRainier on YouTube.

Step 1: **Visualize what life would be like if you had all the willpower you needed.** Close your eyes for a moment, take a slow breath, and imagine your willpower growing, increasing, blossoming until it is a superpower, and you are Willpower Woman or Willpower Man.

In your mind's eye, notice how your superpower is obvious to all.

Step 2: **Take the visualization further: how do you use all your excess Willpower Energy?**

Visualize yourself bursting with Willpower Energy. Your hands are itchy to expend it. Close your eyes again, and visualize it for a moment. Where do you spend it? What do you get done? **Write out 3 specific things you would do if you were bursting with Willpower Energy right now.**

TIPS

Tip 1: Next time you feel you need a willpower boost for a specific task, close your eyes and reimagine yourself bursting with Willpower Energy.

Tip 2: Fun, wasn't it? Try out our Tackling Change course  for more tools to help you reach your future potential.

Visualizations don't help you develop willpower

There are lots of tools that can help you strengthen your willpower, but visualization? That sounds a little too hokey for me.

For:

1. Visualizing the future just sets me up for disappointment. All I see are things I'll never accomplish and a life that looks nothing like my own.
2. Working on my present is more useful than working on my future.
3. I tend to be easily distracted. The more I think about some abstract vision of the future, the less I can focus on my current tasks and responsibilities.

Add you own argument:

4. ____

Against:

1. Visualization motivates me to change what my life looks like and improve my willpower.
2. It may sound morbid but when I visualize my funeral and what I would want people to say about me, I get a lot of clarity of where I should be directing my life and my life goals.
3. Pro athletes are taught to use visualization to their advantage all the time. If it works for them, why shouldn't it work for me?

Add you own argument:

4. ____

9 Things you'll gain when you work on your willpower

Why in the world would you want to spend your time on willpower of all things? There are so many other things you can do with your time. Is it really worth it? Well, enjoy the following examples of what you can gain from willpower, and decide for yourself.

1. Confidence. Because you are working towards attaining a big goal through small, practical, and measurable steps. As each baby goal is accomplished and you can see your progress, your confidence will increase.

2. Determination. If I set my mind to something, and set up a structure to get me there, determination follows suite. There's a way to get there, and now I know what that is, so let me go get it!

3. Motivation. This is the force riding next to willpower in the front seat. If you strengthen your willpower and believe you can do something, motivation will come along for the ride.

4. Excitement. It's fun to see our goals being accomplished, one little step at a time.

5. Inspiration. The further along you get on your journey to obtaining willpower, the more inspiration you'll receive.

6. Admiration. Both from others and yourself. Yes, you got this (and so much more)!

Add your items to the list:

7. ____

8. ____

9. ____

Willpower is a personality thing – either you have it or you don't

From my earliest childhood memories, I can remember struggling with willpower. I definitely would have been one of those kids who failed the Stanford marshmallow experiment. I know working on my willpower is a lost cause…

For:

1. Willpower is a personality trait. You can't change personality traits. At least not easily.
2. Willpower is not a skill that can be fostered. Either you're born with it, or you're not. Period.
3. I don't know anyone who's successfully transformed themselves from willpower-weak to willpower-strong. Why should I think I'm any more special than all the others who have tried and failed?

Add you own argument:

4. ____

Against:

1. Willpower is not a personality thing, it's a skill! A skill is something you cultivate as you grow. And more than that, it's a learned skill. The more you work on it, the greater it will get.
2. Personality traits can also be changed. Everybody changes. In fact, we change ourselves on a daily basis. Just look at the thriving field of self-help for proof!
3. Science and the study of epigenetics show that everything in this world is a two-way street. Willpower is indeed influenced through both nature and nurture.
4. Even if you couldn't change your willpower, you could still learn practical tools of how to best use the willpower you have.

Add you own argument:

5.____

When I envision living with willpower, here's what I see

Living with willpower will certainly create new opportunities. How do you see that having willpower will change things in your life? Where would you pour it? Spend five minutes writing about how you think willpower will change your life in your 'Willpower 101' journal.

Direct message us YOUR story @Buddy_N_Soul on Instagram and be anonymously featured for a chance to **win a Buddy&Soul three month free membership**.

Just deciding to have willpower isn't always enough (just as wanting to change doesn't always translate into results, as most of us know from years of discarded New Year's resolutions). To maintain willpower, you've got to have an authentic goal to fuel your motivation.

In an insightful interview on willpower, author Kelly McGonigal notes that resolutions work when they bring you towards goals that you actually want "for yourself and your life in the next year."

She shared a personal anecdote about a time she asked a colleague if she had made any resolutions. "Oh yeah, to stay fit," the colleague said, but rather unenthusiastically. After a few seconds of silence, though, she added, "I'm kind of thinking about finding a way to play the piano again." At this, McGonigal notes, her colleague started to light up. "It used to be so important to me, and I really miss it. It's like my soul wants to play the piano again, and it would be giving it back to my soul."

To which McGonigal responded, "That's your resolution! What is this getting fit stuff?"

Sometimes, our goals are things that we think we *should* do, and sometimes they are things that we really desire in the long-term. No matter if you want to finally get serious about writing that book you've been dreaming about, or if you need to exercise for health reasons, finding your authentic motivation for your goals will be the accelerator to keep willpower going strong.

(Plus: Check out our Cultivating Authenticity course.) 

Psychologists use an exercise called 'Best Possible Self,' or BPS for short, where you imagine who you want to be in order to bring your goals to the forefront of your mind. The BPS exercise can increase positive future thinking, as demonstrated in a study by Madelon Peters and colleagues, and can help you clarify what you really want. That's one of the secrets to maintaining your willpower.

This doesn't mean that visualizing myself as a respected and accomplished professional will automatically make it happen. Rather, seeing it opens new neural pathways in my brain and primes my body to act in a way that is congruous with my vision.

In plain English, it reminds me that grad school is a real option, so I should stop procrastinating and apply, or that I *can* succeed on the text coming up next week! … So I should probably study. It bridges the gap between my behavior today and my goals for the future.

Envisioning your best possible self will help increase and maintain your motivation – and your willpower.

So, let's take a look at *your* unique willpower goals.

We are happy you've returned, and we're looking forward to deepening our understanding of the motivation behind increasing our willpower. Let's get started!

In order to accomplish something in life, you need motivation. The problem is that motivation is a puzzle which many of us don't understand. We don't know where it comes from, how it influences us and most importantly how to make it on our own.

Career analyst Dan Pink may be able to help us better understand the puzzle that is motivation. You may be surprised at how easily we can use it to our benefit.

Watch 'The Puzzle of Motivation' presented by Dan Pink on YouTube.

Take a few minutes now and write out your vision of your 'Best Possible Self' (BPS) in 5 years' time. Do this in your journal. Note what your ideal life looks like in terms of your work, home life, relationships, lifestyle, or other areas you hope to see improvement in.

Now, let's connect the dots between having willpower and becoming your BPS. **Describe how willpower will help you take action to become your best possible self.** Be concrete and specific. Write your response in your journal.

TIPS

Tip 1: Your reason for wanting to increase your motivation can be anything and everything. Don't worry about it seeming silly, if it's your reason – it is not silly.

Tip 2: Thought of another reason why you want to increase your willpower? You can always come back to your journal and add it in.

Tip 3: For more practical exercises and steps you can take towards your life goals, be sure to check out our Achieve Your Goals course.

If you're like most of us, you signed up for the Willpower 101 course with some concrete goal in mind. Share your key motivator to work on your willpower here. **Spend five minutes writing about** your willpower motivator in your 'Willpower 101' journal.

Direct message us YOUR story @Buddy_N_Soul on Instagram and be anonymously featured for a chance to **win a Buddy&Soul three month free membership**.

7 Best motivators for working on your willpower

Using motivators is a great way to get your willpower muscle pumping. Here are some top motivators we've found to be helpful for us. Be sure to add your own!

1. A loving partner or friend. When I know someone really cares and is concerned for my well-being, I don't want to let them down.
2. A tall iced Frappuccino with whipped cream and caramel on top. Hey, whoever said motivation had to be intrinsic was so wrong. Knowing I have one of those waiting for me almost always guarantees I get the job done.
3. Imagining my success at the end of the day. Success is so tantalizing I can't help push myself to achieve it.
4. Wanting a different home environment than the one I was raised. Thinking back on the past pushes me to change for the future.

Add your items to the list:

5. ____

6. ____

7. ____

What motivates you to work on your willpower?

Motivators are a great way to get your willpower muscles pumping. What are some things that get you motivated to work on your willpower?

1. My past failures. I want to forget about them already.
2. My future. I want things to be better.
3. Loving family and friends. If they believe in me, so can I.
4. Boredom. I want change.
5. Nothing. I'm low on motivation and on willpower.
6. Self-judgement. I want to love myself more.

Did we miss anything? Add it in your journal: ______________________________

How I found motivation for my willpower

When you find that push to keep going, it's like putting willpower on cruise-control. How did you find your motivation—that extra bit of the puzzle that makes everything a little bit easier? Spend five minutes writing about motivation in your 'Willpower 101' journal.

Direct message us YOUR story @Buddy_N_Soul on Instagram and be anonymously featured for a chance to **win a Buddy&Soul three month free membership**.

<u>STRATEGY 4: Understand what depletes your willpower</u>

Maintaining willpower can be challenging, especially when
we view it as a limited resource. This session we will focus
on understanding the depletion of willpower.

Let's start with the all-time example for willpower: food.
Whether or not you are on a strict diet, we all have a limit
to what we can eat. Personally, I love French fries. Every
time I see French fries on the menu I need to keep
reminding myself how unhealthy they are to prevent
myself from ordering them. On those occasions when I
successfully self-regulate and skip the fries, by the time dessert comes around I usually give in to my
other nemesis – chocolate.

Why does this happen? **Am I just rewarding myself for not ordering the fries, or is there more to it?**

According to social psychologist Roy Baumeister, people have limited mental resources that get used up
throughout the day. This phenomenon is referred to as ego depletion. This means that if you were
spending the whole day resisting saying something rude to a coworker, you would have a harder time
resisting saying something a little harsh to your partner after getting home.

Why is that? Similar to any other muscle in your body, the willpower muscle tires as you use it. By the
time evening comes around, it's usually a bit sore and not functioning as it would in the morning.

Let's take a look at a study conducted by Baumeister and his colleagues to explore this. Study
participants were divided into two groups. One group was instructed to eat cookies and the other
radishes, both in the same room. The cookie-eaters saw the radishes but could not eat them, and
likewise – if you were assigned to eating radishes – the fresh cookies were right there, smelling great,
but not for you. About five minutes after eating, each participant was asked to solve a persistence-
testing puzzle.

Interestingly, they found that the radish-eating participants made fewer attempts and devoted less than
half the time to solving the puzzle, as compared to the cookie-eating participants. In other words, the
participants who resisted the cookies had less mental resources while solving the puzzle since their
willpower had already been somewhat depleted. They had less self-control to exert.

Understanding that willpower is limited can help you prioritize your choices and consider where you can
give your willpower muscle a break. This way, you can save all that mental muscle for where you need it
most.

We are in the midst of building our willpower. Like any other resource in your body, your willpower can be strengthened as well as depleted.

Think of your willpower as a muscle. Becoming aware of this causes us to think twice about how and when we flex this particular muscle, and to consider if there are things we should do to keep our willpower muscle strong, and perhaps things to avoid to keep it from tiring out.

In the talk we're about to see, psychologist Roy Baumeister introduces the idea of the willpower muscle, and will deepen our understanding of how it works.

As you watch, try to identify moments in your daily routine when you inadvertently deplete some of your willpower.

Watch 'Willpower: Self-Control, Decision Fatigue, and Energy' presented by Roy Baumeister on YouTube.

EXERCISE

Imagine you are the 'wasted willpower police' searching for areas in your day where your willpower is discarded needlessly. For example, working with the TV on forces you to resist getting distracted, which wastes some of the willpower you could have used to get your work done. **What do you think would be your top wasted willpower crime?** Write it down in your journal.

Next, think of creative ways to cut back on the need for willpower in such situations and write them down in the second textbox. For example: Allow yourself 30 minutes of uninterrupted TV time instead of trying to watch while working.

TIPS

Tip 1: Not quite sure how to allocate your time, energy, and willpower? Check out our Priorities Reboot  course to help you clarify the big things in your life.

Tip 2: Come back to your journal and keep track of how much willpower energy you are saving. You can even try thinking of it as a game!

Tip 3: Make yourself a digital badge, to remind yourself when you're on the clock as a top detective for the WWPD.

Willpower is NOT a muscle

Muscles are physical parts of our body that we can see. Willpower is an imaginative concept. They are not the same!

For:

1. If willpower is a muscle, then give it a fancy Latin name and tell me where to find it on the human body.
2. If I want to work on my willpower, I go to psychologist and not to a personal trainer.
3. The metaphor is cute but let's face it: willpower always stays the same. Unlike muscle tone, you can't develop willpower just because you want to.

Add your own argument:

4. ____

Against:

1. Just like a muscle, our willpower can be strengthened, weakened, flexed, challenged, and strained.
2. If it acts like a duck, walks like a duck and quacks like a duck… well, it's most likely a duck.
3. Physically, no, it is not a muscle. But just like the tongue *is* a muscle that you don't exercise to make stronger (unless you're auditioning for Lafayette on *Hamilton*), willpower is a non-muscle you *can* exercise and make stronger.

Add your own argument:

4. ____

12 Ways to reduce your exposure to willpower-depleting temptations

Planning ahead when it comes to temptations can help you avoid them altogether. Here are a few tips for minimizing your exposure to temptations.

1. Identify your temptations. Before you go anywhere, ask yourself if you will come in contact with something that you do not want to eat, drink, buy, or smoke. If the answer is yes, try to find a different locale!
2. Rid your home of junk food and stock up on healthy (and tasty) snacks.
3. If you are trying to lose weight, avoid eating out at restaurants and fast food joints where you don't know what is put into the food you order.
4. If you are tempted by alcohol, forgo hanging out with friends at a bar, or make it your mission to try out—and rank—all the virgin cocktails. You might even volunteer to be the designated driver!
5. Distance yourself from the friends who will peer pressure you into doing something you do not want to do, and stay close with those who are invested in helping you kick habits and lead a healthy life.
6. Shut off your computer for a few hours each day. One of the biggest temptations is to just surf the internet all day. Shutting off the computer (or detaching your palm from your phone) will ensure that you will have at least a few productive hours.
7. If you are working on kicking a cigarette addiction, avoid stores that sell cigarettes and people who use them.
8. Cancel your credit cards (or at least leave them at home). Paying with cash or debit will really limit your expenditures!
9. At the end of the day you need to live your life. At some point or another you will be exposed to a temptation. Exercising your willpower and fighting off urges will increase your chances of successfully fighting them off again next time around!

Add your items to the list:

10. ____

11. ____

12. ____

Willpower failures only makes you stronger for the next time.

They say that "whatever doesn't kill you only makes you stronger." Well, maybe that applies to my never-ending willpower struggles too. Do my failed attempts at willpower do anything for me in the long run?

For:

1. When you know what it feels like to fail – and it doesn't feel very good – you are more motivated to avoid failure the next time around. You will be more likely to exercise your willpower to the fullest extent.
2. Setbacks help you fine-tune your strategies. You'll be better prepared to ace it next time.
3. Failing makes you realize how much you want to succeed. This idea will be a motivating factor the next time a temptation arises.
4. Each attempt to exercise willpower builds your muscles. It doesn't matter if you ultimately cave – the important thing is that you pushed yourself. Next time, you'll push yourself just a little bit more. And then the time after that, a little more still.

Add your own argument:

5. ____

Against:

1. Willpower failures will leave you feeling discouraged. If you failed this time, then what's preventing you from failing again in the future?
2. Willpower failures will make you feel like you can never succeed, which will cause you to just ignore the issue and never try to tackle it again.
3. When you have a willpower failure, it could cause your support system to fall apart. People will stop believing in you and your ability to succeed.

Add your own argument:

4. ____

The moment I knew my willpower had been depleted

In those times when you just can't keep it up anymore, you realize that your willpower has been depleted. When did you realize that this had happened to you, and what did you do about it? Spend five minutes writing about depleted willpower in your 'Willpower 101' journal.

Direct message us YOUR story @Buddy_N_Soul on Instagram and be anonymously featured for a chance to **win a Buddy&Soul three month free membership**.

When we talk about willpower as a muscle, our minds may naturally conjure up images of Schwarzenegger-esque body builders working under top trainers, pumping mass amounts of iron and sweating buckets.

Or maybe it's just me…

In any case, it's easy to think, "That's for the pros," or, "Oh, I'll never get there." But in fact, the research on developing willpower paints a much more modest picture.

Instead of Schwarzenegger pumping iron, you would be more aligned with the science if you envisioned a regular person you know – or even yourself – walking one lap around the living room each day.

For example, in her book *The Willpower Instinct,* Stanford health psychologist Kelly McGonigal writes about the power of committing to a small act of self-control, like cutting back on sweets or improving your posture.

These seemingly insignificant tasks may appear unimportant when it comes to the bigger willpower challenges, but it turns out that they do improve your overall inner strength.

As an example, McGonigal presents a study conducted at Northwestern University that tested this notion with two weeks of willpower training to reduce violence against romantic partners.

In the study, a group of participants was asked to change small habits in their day, such as using their non-dominant hand for tasks, or saying "yes" instead of "yeah." After two weeks, this group showed a reduction in physical violence as a response to typical triggering events, in comparison to the control group. Meaning, the simple acts they were asked to execute for two weeks strengthened their overall self-discipline and they were less likely to lose control. Their willpower muscle had become stronger.

Most of us don't respond with violence when we lose control. But we each have situations where we need to overcome the temptation to respond inappropriately. The simple act of training the self-control muscle, even by committing to a small exercise, gives us more willpower.

Why is that?

When we train our brains to pause and notice what we are about to do, we prevent automatic responses. Am I going to put one or two spoons of honey in my tea? Which hand will I use to eat breakfast? Although these tasks can be challenging at times, they are not overwhelming, and are less likely to trigger strong feelings. Little by little, small and mundane tasks will help you increase your willpower.

As you may recall, we recently learned that willpower functions like a muscle. Although it means that our willpower depletes throughout the day, it also means that we can strengthen it, little by little. In the following clip, Stanford health psychologist Kelly McGonigal speaks about willpower as a bodily process and how we can use this to our advantage. In the action bit that follows, we'll be looking at the power of small steps in helping you pump up your willpower.

Watch 'The Willpower Instinct' presented by Kelly McGonigal on YouTube.

Right now, take note of your posture, and sit up straight for one full minute on the clock. As you're doing that, **take an awesome-posture selfie and upload it to Instagram** to serve as your reminder that by actively exercising self-control in any area, you'll strengthen your overall willpower.

Post your picture on Instagram and Twitter, tagging @Buddy_N_Soul, and Facebook @Buddy&Soul using the hashtag #BuddynSoulWellness. By sharing with us on social media, not only can you help others with their personal journeys, you can read about those facing similar challenges.

TIPS

Tip 1: Although the idea that a simple task can increase your willpower seems silly, try it – for a week, or longer. It'll pay off.

Tip 2: Keep your willpower exercises gentle and fun so they don't tire you out for your regular responsibilities.

Tip 3: Come back to your journal and update how far you've come with strengthening your willpower muscle.

13 Empowering ideas to help build your willpower

Let's face it – building willpower is exhausting! If you're having a hard time keeping up your motivation, have a look at these insights about willpower and recharge.

1. There's "I won't" power, "I will" power, and "I want" power working together as a team, influencing our willpower. The more we want something, the greater our ability will be to will it into being.
2. Willpower is like intelligence. It's a general strength that can improve anything.
3. Willpower can predict how successful I will be in the future; a better predictor than even intelligence!
4. Willpower is about remembering what our goals are and following through on them.
   (Plus: Check out our Achieve Your Goals course.)
5. Willpower is thinking long-term satisfaction, as opposed to short-term instant gratification.
6. When I use willpower in my relationships, I can focus more on my partner and friends and give them the attention they deserve.
7. It makes sense that my willpower muscle gets tired a lot; the society we live in offers non-stop temptations.
8. By controlling our impulses with our willpower, we can live a life geared to accomplishing our goals.
9. Sleeping at night does not mean I'm lazy. It means recharging your willpower in order to function healthfully!
10. Meditating and mindfulness grow the area of the brain that controls willpower. Our willpower muscle *can* be strengthened.
    (Plus: Check out our Mindfulness for Beginners course.)

Add your items to the list:

11. ____

12. ____

13. ____

11 Signs that your willpower is like a muscle

Even though willpower is an abstract skill, it functions very similarly to a physical muscle. Here are a few examples.

1. When you stop exercising and practicing your willpower, it will become flabby and weak.
2. When you push your muscles to their limit they get stronger. The more you use your willpower, the stronger it will be.
3. If you push your muscles too far they will be strained and injured. If put on overdrive, willpower can be exhausted and damaged. Sometimes you need to allow yourself to have some fun.
4. Just like eating healthy and exercising are good for your muscles, leading a healthy lifestyle nurtures your brain and gives it the inner strength to utilize willpower effectively.
5. You use your muscles to accomplish many types of tasks. Willpower will help you succeed in all aspects of your life.
6. Sometimes you treat your muscles to a gift – a massage! Give yourself a gift and a pat on the back when you have successfully used willpower to accomplish something.
7. Just like muscles cannot function without ligaments and bones, willpower cannot be employed without self-awareness, patience and perseverance.
8. There are no shortcuts to getting big muscles. It is hard and tiring work! Building up your willpower is tiring and hard as well, but will lead to lasting results.

Add your items to the list:

9. ____

10. ____

11. ____

Dealing with minor obstacles helps build willpower for greater tasks.

Runners train to prepare themselves for a marathon. Similarly, minor obstacles are like training races. They'll prepare you for bigger willpower challenges that come your way.

For:

1. Tackling minor challenges will sharpen your problem-solving skills. By the time a huge challenge comes along, you'll have had ample practice dealing with tough situations.
2. Dealing with minor challenges will build your confidence to face your challenges head-on.
3. Getting minor obstacles out of the way will give you the time and the energy to focus on the greater challenges.

Add you own argument:

4. ____

Against:

1. Major obstacles are nothing like minor obstacles. When you encounter the real deal, you're not going to know what hit you.
2. Being able to deal with minor obstacles by yourself may prevent you from seeking assistance when a big challenge comes along. After all, willpower is finite and you might need someone else to help you supplement your limited supply.
3. After successfully overcoming temptations or minor obstacles, you develop a false hope that you can easily deal with any challenge that comes your way. When a major obstacle comes along, you will be discouraged when dealing with it isn't as manageable.

Add you own argument:

4. ____

The surprising thing I did to strengthen my willpower muscle

Thinking of willpower as a muscle is empowering and also opens up a new range of possibilities for how to use and strengthen it. Describe what you've found helpful in learning to strengthen your willpower muscle. Spend five minutes writing about strengthening your willpower muscle in your 'Willpower' journal.

Direct message us YOUR story @Buddy_N_Soul on Instagram and be anonymously featured for a chance to **win a Buddy&Soul three month free membership**.

Not too long ago, I decided to go for a morning run every day. At the time, it seemed like an easy goal. All I needed to do was get up and get out the door. Six months later, I still haven't started my magical morning exercise.

I know I'm human, but I can't help wondering whether I could have done something differently to enable me to succeed.

In their bestselling book *Nudge,* Nobel Prize winner Richard Thaler and professor Cass Sunstein introduce the idea of nudging ourselves to make more sensible choices. "A nudge, as we will use the term, is any aspect of the choice architecture that alters people's behavior in a predictable way without forbidding any options or significantly changing their economic incentives" (p. 6).

A nudge can be as simple as setting an alarm clock for your morning walk or making sure you have fresh vegetables in the fridge to cut a salad. This idea presumes that you are your own choice architect. Meaning, you decide how to design your choice environment, what kind of nudges you prepare and how subtle (or not) they are. Nudges catapult us towards the action that we want to do anyway without depleting our willpower.

Thaler and Sunstein claim that many predictable problems arise when people need to delay gratification, which tests their capacity for self-discipline. This, they say, is particularly true when the consequence does not immediately follow the choice.

For example, will you get out of bed to floss your teeth if you realize you've forgotten to? The consequence of missing flossing for one night might seem insignificant at the time – and emerging from your cozy cocoon would require a heavy dose of willpower. If you look at the big picture, though, *habitual* not-flossing can have a serious impact on your teeth in the long run. And we know that every slippery slope starts with a single downhill step.

So, what can you do to steer yourself in the direction of making the willpowered choice? Nudge yourself!

The difference can be as simple as keeping an extra roll of dental floss on your nightstand. **Find nudges that you can enforce daily, to ease your willpower challenges.** Because nudges require less willpower, it will be easier and more enjoyable to reach your goals.

Make these no-nonsense nudges, so that you don't have any room to bargain with yourself.

We are here to change and become more 'willpowered.' The question is – how? The problem is that so many willpower-building techniques are rather drastic and bombastic, and we tend to forget about them after a week or two. Is there a simpler, longer-lasting and more effective way to approach willpower?

According to behavioral designer (yes, it's a thing) Sille Krukow, there is. She claims that nudging is the way to go. According to Krukow, changing actual human behavior calls for good design solutions that take basic human instincts, flaws, and habits into consideration. You may be surprised how easily you can reduce the need for willpower in your life.

Watch 'Design to Nudge and Change Behaviour' presented by Sillie Krukow at TEDxCopenhagen on YouTube.

Create one nudge that enables you to circumvent the need for willpower in one area of your life. For example, if making healthy eating choices demands a lot of willpower for you, consider adding 'fresh salad greens' as a permanent item to your weekly shopping list, or committing to spending ten minutes every Sunday morning cutting up fruits and veggies so that you'll have healthy snacks on hand, at least for the first half of the week. Write your idea for a nudge in your journal.

TIPS

Tip 1: Interested in furthering your knowledge of how to come about changing your habits? Check out our Habit Workshop course.

Tip 2: Nudges turn great choices into a no-brainer. Incorporate them freely in your routine.

Nudges are fantastic tools to help guide you towards the behavior you want. By setting yourself up in advance, you're basically cutting out the middle-man who keeps getting in the way: You.

When you don your running clothes first thing in the morning, it's a little silly *not* to go for a run, right?

Except sometimes we surprise ourselves in our ability to find loopholes in our own contracts.

What are some of the nudges that failed you? How did you get around them, and what would you need to do differently for them to work, next time? Share your story of failed nudges with the community, and help others learn from your experience! Spend five minutes writing about nudges that failed you in your 'Willpower 101' journal.

Direct message us YOUR story @Buddy_N_Soul on Instagram and be anonymously featured for a chance to **win a Buddy&Soul three month free membership**.

13 Nudge ideas to help circumvent your willpower

If only we could get moving whenever we wanted to… well with a helpful 'nudge,' or a kick in the butt, as we called it in my house, we can get ourselves moving at a much faster pace. Here are some nudges that

can get you moving before you even realize that your willpower is at play.

1. Wear your running clothes first thing in the morning; you'll also be half-way there towards your run, and you'll be advertising your intent to everyone who sees you. That's basically a public promise you've made, and are more likely to keep.
2. Set a reward *before* you make the effort. That way you know you're working towards something.
3. Select a playlist to listen to while you work or study, so you're less inclined to put on the TV for "background noise" and *ooh, I love this part and*—well, you know.
4. Partnering with a buddy for some or all of your goals. Knowing they're outside waiting is a great way to get up and go.
5. Having a friend call or text me. It makes me feel accountable for my actions. And inaction.
6. Deleting numbers of all fast-food delivery places on my phone. It's like a backward nudge because I'm not going to bother looking up a number again.
7. Posting my plans on social media. Once others know, I feel more accountable.
8. Locking unwanted items away from my immediate reach—unhealthy snacks, distracting crafts projects, etc.
9. Eating a healthy meal before I go out. My full tummy nudges me not to order more food, and certainly not the amount I'd have ordered, otherwise.
10. Laying out all the books, notes, dictionaries and articles I need to study properly tomorrow. Getting the materials ready is half the battle.

Add your items to the list:

11. ____

12. ____

13. ____

Which nudges help you with your willpower?

Sometimes wanting something isn't enough to get our willpower rolling. Giving our willpower a little nudge, however, can motivate us. Which nudges have you found helpful?

1. Setting a reward *before* I make the effort.
2. Having a playlist ready, so I listen to music instead of having the TV on when studying or working.
3. Having a friend call/text me.
4. Posting my plans on social media. Once others know I feel more accountable.
5. Locking unwanted items away from my immediate reach.
6. Laying out the items I need in advance. When I'm doing it it's not a commitment, and when I'm ready to begin working half the battle is already fought.

Did we miss anything? Add it in your journal: ___________________________________

How one little nudge did wonders for my willpower

Nudges are small and powerful, often transforming our lives by making a hard thing easier. Which nudge did you implement that made it easier to maintain your willpower? share it here, and maybe inspire others to adopt your nudge! Spend five minutes writing about nudges in your 'Willpower 101' journal.

Direct message us YOUR story @Buddy_N_Soul on Instagram and be anonymously featured for a chance to **win a Buddy&Soul three month free membership**.

Living in the modern world, we're called upon to make choices in an ever-changing, fast-paced environment on moment-by-moment basis. Whether regarding the heavy hitters – like finances, work, and schooling – or the more everyday choices – like what to eat, wear, or buy – the options often seem endless. And almost all of them require at least some level of willpower!

Take a look at food, for instance. There are hundreds, if not thousands, of options for every meal or snack, and if health is a priority, you hope to choose an apple over a Snickers bar. Even a small decision like that uses willpower, and you are making hundreds of such decisions each day.

We want to make the right choices, and one way to do that is by understanding how our brain works. So let's have a look at the science behind your willpower.

According to *The Willpower Instinct,* willpowered decision-making takes place in three regions of the prefrontal cortex of the brain. And each region has its own specialty:

1. **"I will" power**: The first region of the prefrontal cortex helps you stick to boring, stressful, or difficult tasks (laundry, anyone?).
2. **"I won't" power:** The second region holds you back from following every craving or impulse you may have (e.g., no more donuts this week).
3. **"I want" power**: The third region keeps track of your goals and desires, basically what YOU want to achieve in the long run. This region reminds you what you really want, even when your temptations are staring at you and all you want to do is to cave and buy that pair of boots or smoke that one-more cigarette.

In fact, in the words of Kelly McGonigal, "The development of willpower – I will, I won't and I want – may define what it means to be human."

A study published in PNAS found something similar: that cigarette craving was eliminated when the dorsal part of the prefrontal context was de-activated.

But, don't use this as an excuse, as in 'I can't help my prefrontal cortex!' because you can. You can change your brain with new thinking patterns.

Having your "I want" power in mind when making decisions and exercising your willpower muscle will make it easier to choose the harder option. So while it may be super difficult for me to *not* have that Snickers bar, and a million excuses have already popped into mind to justify it, resisting it becomes easier if I remind myself that *I **want** to feel good about myself this evening*. The faster this region fires its cells, and the more you want something, the more motivated you are to take action. So, remind yourself of your "I want" to fire your brain cells faster, keeping you motivated and driven.

DRIVING THE MESSAGE HOME

Success is something we all dream of, but have a hard time believing is possible. Does this hurt our chances of succeeding? According to entrepreneur Carrie Green, it does; our mindset has a significant impact on whether we succeed in life.

We are responsible for the state of our minds, which is a rather large responsibility. So why not take this state of mind and program it to our advantage?

In the action that follows, we will do just that, learning some of the neuroscience behind willpower and how to spin it in our favor.

Without further ado, here it is.

Watch 'Programming Your Mind For Success' presented by Carrie Green at TEDxManchester on YouTube.

Complete each of the following statements in light of what we've just learned about willpower:

- Today, **I will**: _________________ (e.g. an important but boring task)
- Today, **I won't**: _________________ (e.g. a bad habit you want to break)
- Today, **I want**: _________________ (e.g. something that would make you happy, to counter the *won't* power.)

Write your responses in your journal and then – most importantly – make these things happen!

TIPS

Tip 1: Let your imagination go wild! Don't hold back on what you would like to accomplish.

Tip 2: Come back and reread what you wrote at the end of the day. How did you do? If you liked the feeling, consider turning these wills, won'ts, and wants into daily habits.

(Plus: Check out our Habit Workshop course.) 

Tip 3: Nothing is too small, or too embarrassing, to write down.

How I reprogrammed my mind for success

Neuroscience has taught us that we are constantly changing our brains. What are you doing to reprogram your mind for success? Share your ideas, tricks and tips below. Spend five minutes writing about your experience reprograming your mind for success in your 'Willpower 101' journal.

Direct message us YOUR story @Buddy_N_Soul on Instagram and be anonymously featured for a chance to **win a Buddy&Soul three month free membership**.

11 Things in your life that are worth cultivating 'want-power' for

The power of want is really the motivation factor in willpower. Why shouldn't you have that cookie? Not because it's unhealthy, and not because it's calorically rich, but because you *want to feel good about yourself.* Identifying why you want something is the best way to stick to the plan. Here are some ideas for *want* behind the changes we make.

1. I don't want to "lose weight", I want to **look nice**. That's the goal I'm working towards.

2. I don't really care about updating these specific spreadsheets at work, but I should put in the extra hours because I want to **earn the promotion.**

3. I don't want to stop smoking. I love smoking. What I want is to **stop coughing at the sight of a flight of stairs.**

4. I have no passion for my last two Pol-Sci credits on the Cuban Missile Crisis. But what I *want* is a **career change**, and I need this degree to make that happen.

5. I don't want to stop comparing myself to others. That's a fun, if terrible destructive, game to play. But what I do want is to **be more content with the life I lead.** That's why I will stop playing "Hotter than Me" on the train.

6. I don't like running. I think that to so-called "endorphin high" is a classic example of folie à deux (or the many). I never *want* to run. But that's okay. Because what I want is to **enjoy guilt-free cookies,** so if I have to exercise to earn them—I can pay that price.

7. I am never in the mood to move the sofa, put up tarps, and pain. But what I want is to **have a put-together, welcoming home**. That's why I will completing my home improvement projects.

8. Do I want to turn off the TV, after a long day at work, and make phone calls? Take a wild stab. But I *do* want to **stay in touch with my friends and family**, and let them know that I think about them. That's why I'll get up and make those calls. Tags:

Add your items to the list:

9. ____

10. ____

11. ____

Well, never say never, but let's face it – it's harder to put some things on the backburner than others. What are some bad habits you're just not ready to part with at this point?

1. My late/non-existent bedtime.
2. My cigarettes. There's always a rationalization for one more.
3. Coffee, coffee, and more coffee.
4. My smartphone addiction.
5. Poor eating habits – I'm just not the sugar-free, carb-free, gluten-free-ice-diet type!

Did we miss anything? Add it in your journal: _______________________________

How the "I will" mindset improved my willpower

Your "I will" power is a part of your willpower and it's a tool that can help you persevere. Share the commitment you made and how you got there with the "I will" mindset. Inspire the rest of us to follow your lead! Spend five minutes writing about the "I will" mindset in your 'Willpower 101' journal.

Direct message us YOUR story @Buddy_N_Soul on Instagram and be anonymously featured for a chance to **win a Buddy&Soul three month free membership**.

Many of us, myself included, have a tendency to justify our lack of self-discipline by using sensible reasoning. "I'm working on my day off, so why shouldn't I eat those chocolate covered pecans?" Or, "Pecans are healthy, even if they are covered in sugar."

Many times, we feel it's okay to do something 'wrong' if we pair it with something 'right.'

It's almost as if the virtue gives us moral license to engage in the vice. Eating chocolate after a jog, vegging out in front of the TV after a long work day, or leaving the dishes since I already did a major cleaning today. Don't we deserve it?

The answer is yes, we do deserve to give our willpower a rest once in a while, and reward ourselves. It's only problematic when rewarding ourselves causes us to undo what we have accomplished until that point. As if taking one step forward gives us permission to take two steps back. Or sideways.

In a paper titled *Moral Self Licensing: When Being Good Frees Us to Be Bad*, researchers describe how we do just that, in areas such as ethical behaviour, but also consumer choice.

For example, in one study, researchers asked half the participants to imagine doing something altruistic, and unquestionably good, such as doing volunteer work. Then they asked the participants to make a hypothetical choice between buying a luxury good such as designer jeans, and a necessity, such as a vacuum cleaner. As you can probably guess, the do-gooders were more inclined to choose the luxury item than those who did not 'earn' the moral license to indulge.

It's easy to see how 'I worked out so hard' can translate into a moral license to binge on the ice cream carton in the freezer. Poof. All gone.

Except ice cream isn't 'bad,' and you can enjoy it without polishing off the entire container.

Is there a way to indulge without undoing all the hard work we have put into strengthening our willpower?

The answer is a resounding YES! But it involves setting some ground rules for yourself.

That means that *before* you indulge in your well-deserved reward, you clearly define your terms. You know exactly when and how much you allow yourself to indulge and then you stick to the plan one hundred percent.

Ironically, even though keeping to the rules requires willpower, it actually puts far less strain on your overall willpower bank.

So, three spoons of ice cream after work? Yay! An entire pint whenever you so desire? Not so much.

We all have a moral code, which may or may not allow us to behave in certain ways. According to behavioral economist (yup, it's a real thing) Dan Ariely there are small bugs in our moral code which make us feel okay with slightly stretching our moral limits.

What does this have to do with willpower? Well, there are times we cheat at willpower. We may not want to admit this, but we can't be in control 24/7. In order for us to be in control of how, when and if we cheat, we must understand our moral code.

Watch 'Our Buggy Moral Code' presented by Dan Ariely on YouTube.

Create a rule for your indulgences. Write down one indulgence that you would like to give into and set the conditions for how you can allow this indulgence, and how often.

For example, because I cannot afford distractions when I study, I'll withstand the temptation and then indulge in watching a movie on the weekend.

TIPS

Tip 1: A reward doesn't need to cost money; it can something small and free like a soothing bath or a walk through the local nature reserve.

Tip 2: Remove temptation. If your rule allows three spoons of ice cream, put them in a nice bowl and then promptly return the container to the freezer.

Ethics and morals have nothing to do with willpower

Willpower is about exerting your inner strength and self-control. What in the world does that have to do with your morals, values, and ethical code?

For:

1. Willpower, or your capacity to persevere, is a skill, not a value. Sure, it can be *paired* with values to create a well-prioritized life, but in and of itself, no, it has nothing to do with ethics.
2. Throughout history, people have used willpower to perform atrocious acts. What does that teach us about willpower's connection to ethics and morals?

Add you own argument:

3. ____

Against:

1. If willpower is about perseverance, it makes sense that it would be easier to maintain in situations aligned with your values.
2. When our behavior and values contradict, we try to reconcile the cognitive dissonance by making excuses for our behavior. So, ethics and morals do have to do with willpower – and might help us examine those excuses and get back on the bandwagon when we slack off.
3. You've got to align your desire to have willpower with your ethics and morals if you want to be able to maintain it. Willpower has to come from an authentic place inside you.

Add you own argument:

4. ____

How helpful is each of these in replenishing your willpower?

Working on your willpower is tiring, and in order to persevere you need to replenish yourself. How helpful do you find each of these as tools for replenishing your willpower?

1. Exercising.
2. Prayer or other spiritual practice.
3. Sleep.
4. Eating well.
5. Rewarding myself with a treat for a job well done.
6. Watching my favorite show or movie.
7. Hanging out on social media.

Did we miss anything? Add it in your journal: _______________________________

14 Ways to replenish your willpower

If you are feeling low on willpower, it is time to boost it up. How? Here are some ideas; pick what is right for you, and replenish your energy.

1. Sleep. Willpower is like the proverbial ignored middle child when you're tired.
2. Chocolate. Not sure it's scientifically valid, but it can't harm.
3. Plan the night before. Leave your gym bag by the door and book a class in advance. It helps when it is already booked and in the schedule.
4. Have a buddy.
5. Do things in small increments. A day, a week, or a month. It all takes practice. Saturday can be your 'Unplugging day or afternoon' and Tuesday can be your 'No snacks day.'
6. Put it in the schedule. Create a sense of commitment, even for abstract goals.
7. Feign fear (or make it real) of the consequences. Just don't take it too far.
8. Pretend you have no choices or no budget for that vice.
9. As well as sleep, make sure you're fed and watered. Never go shopping or make big decisions on an empty stomach.
10. Find a different distraction. A friend learned to crochet so she could do something with her hands instead of holding a cigarette.
11. And... don't forget to cut yourself some slack. Willpower isn't linear; it will wax and wane like the moon above, just keep using it that mental muscle.

Add your items to the list:

12. ____

13. ____

14. ____

Sometimes all it takes is a very small fix to replenish willpower. What is your secret weapon for persevering when your willpower has been depleted? Spend five minutes writing about replenishing willpower in your 'Willpower 101' journal.

Direct message us YOUR story @Buddy_N_Soul on Instagram and be anonymously featured for a chance to **win a Buddy&Soul three month free membership**.

Sometimes we fall off the wagon. When that happens, we might be inclined to throw in the towel, because the experience of failure is so painful.

For example, if I'm already distressed because I ate an extra donut, eating three more donuts may feel inconsequential. After all, I'm already in the painful and shaky place of "failure."

This is what's called the What-The-Hell effect – and believe it or not, this is rooted in behavioural economics.

Psychologists Amos Tversky and Nobel Prize winner Daniel Kahneman explain this idea at length in a paper on the theory of loss aversion. They demonstrate that the emotional pain of losing is almost twice as powerful as the pleasure of gaining, which is why people would rather avoid losses than obtain gains.

Here's how loss aversion plays out.

Researchers from the Institute of Neurology at the University College London conducted an experiment where they gave each participant $50 and two options: keep $20 or gamble with a 50/50 chance of keeping or losing the whole amount. Less than half of the participants (43%) chose to gamble.

Then, the research team gave participants a second $50 and two new options: Lose $30 for sure, or gamble with a 50/50 chance of keeping or losing the whole amount. Now, over half the participants (61%) chose to gamble. While the scenarios were essentially the same (keeping $20 is the same as losing $30), the subtle difference was in the semantics. The word 'lose' triggered an increase in gambling because people hate to lose! They prefer gambling and risking an additional loss, but also having the chance of getting out of the painful loss domain, to incurring a certain loss of $30.

Loss aversion can weaken our ability to get back on the wagon and persevere after a willpower blip.

My sense of disappointment after losing self-control and eating one donut is already wreaking havoc, so what's three more? After all, I'm already in the loss domain.

What can we do to minimize the impact of loss aversion when we have a willpower failure? We can prepare ourselves ahead of time to accept failure as a learning experience, and realize that it's a part of life. Lack of self-discipline might hurt, but that feeling will pass and we don't have to let it stop us.

Before the loss of willpower occurs, plan your response so you don't end up running with the failure or loss and saying 'who cares anymore'. Decide that you will brush yourself off and jump back on the wagon, because there's so much more to gain.

DRIVING THE MESSAGE HOME

Fear is a feeling we are all familiar with. One kind of fear is the fear of losing, or in our case, the fear of failing at willpower. According to award-winning rocket scientist, science entertainer, and educator Olympia LePoint, we must reprogram our brains to overcome the fear. Otherwise, it might hurt our chances at success.

This session will be about preparing yourself for a willpower failure and knowing how to get yourself back on the wagon after a slip-up.

The more prepared we feel, the better we'll be at handling fear when it tries to get in our way.

Watch 'Reprogramming your Brain to Overcome Fear' presented by Olympia LePoint at TEDxPCC on YouTube.

Imagine a wise stranger handing you a fortune cookie with custom-tailored advice to help you get right back on the willpower wagon after a slip-up.

What would the great advice be that would enable you to get back on?

Examples might be, "If I fail to go on my morning jog I will do a home workout instead of giving up altogether." Or "If skip my drawing class on Sunday, I will still commit to creating one new sketch before next week's class."

TIPS

Tip 1: When you feel your willpower dwindling, take a moment to recharge and breathe slowly before you act. Unless your house is burning down, everything can wait until you give yourself a moment, or two, or three.

Tip 2: Check out our Declutter Your Mind course   to clear out some of the negative messages that might linger when you experience failure.

6 Hacks for overcoming fear

Fear signals challenge, and that in of itself is not a bad thing. Here are some ideas to get through the fear and move on with harnessing your willpower for the things that are important to you.
(Plus: Check out our Priorities Reboot course.)

1. Think of the most fearless person you know and pretend you are them until you've aced the situation fearlessly.
2. Consider what underlines your fear and figure out how you can resolve that issue, so that you can face the task head on.
3. Figure out what message you can tell yourself that will soothe you, and repeat it to yourself until you believe it.

Add your items to the list:

4. ____

5. ____

6. ____

Willpower is hard. Period. You can make it a little easier by being aware of unnecessary obstacles in your way so you can choose to take a different path.

1. Previous failures. Yes, you may have tried to get in shape easily over a hundred times – or at least said you were going to try. You need to dismiss these previous failures as utterly irrelevant and start with a blank slate.
2. Unsupportive friends, family, or coworkers. It can be really hard to push yourself and work on your willpower when the people around you are totally not supportive of your changes. Know that your willpower is totally not affected by their bad mojo.
3. Exhaustion. It's incredibly challenging to try to make a change in anything, let alone willpower, when you're exhausted beyond your means. Make sure you give yourself a week (or two, or three) to fill up your gas tank. You can only make it to the finish line if you're driving on full and not empty.
4. Disorganization. If you are unable to make an organized plan of action, it is going to be much harder to get there. Don't let your goals fall by the wayside with all the chaos in your life.
5. Generalizing. There's no quicker way to bring yourself down than by generalizing your failures. That means that every time you mess up, you say things to yourself like, "There I go again!" or, "I guess this is just who I am!" A much healthier and more productive approach is to *localize* it, e.g., "I'm generally pretty capable, but boy did I mess up this time!"

Add your items to the list:

6. ____

7. ____

8. ____

Willpower training is for people who have strong willpower to begin with

It's like anything in life – the straight A students are the ones who show up for extra math help and the top employees are the ones who attend the lunchtime professional development workshops. Same with willpower. For those who are really in need, a course on willpower isn't going to do too much.

For:

1. Buildings with stronger foundations are able to withstand more. This is true for willpower too. The more innate willpower you have to begin with, the stronger your willpower will become with training.
2. Willpower training is easier when it's not an altogether new skill. That way, when you start working on it, you aren't reinventing the wheel; you're just sharpening the tools you already possess.
3. You have the willpower to stay committed to improving your willpower!

Add you own argument:

4. ____

Against:

1. If you know your willpower is weak, you will likely be more open to learning about and working on it.
2. Willpower training works well for people from all backgrounds and starting points. It doesn't matter where you fall on the spectrum, it just matters that you're moving in the right direction.
3. Even Arnold Schwarzenegger wasn't born with fully formed Mr. World muscles. In fact, he couldn't even hold up his own head for the first few weeks of life. So cut yourself some slack, too. You can build your willpower muscles, even if you're coming a little late to the game.

Add you own argument:

4. ____

There are so many ways to remind ourselves to keep going despite failures. What was a great piece of advice that worked for you when you encountered a willpower blip? Share it with the community and let us get inspired too! Spend five minutes writing about getting back on the willpower in your 'Willpower 101' journal.

Direct message us YOUR story @Buddy_N_Soul on Instagram and be anonymously featured for a chance to **win a Buddy&Soul three month free membership**.

STRATEGY 10: Track your willpower wins

We started this course with a discussion about your goals, with the understanding that developing your willpower will help you achieve them. As we end the course, I want to share another benefit that comes along with willpower – and that is future success.

In his now-classic Stanford marshmallow experiment, Walter Mischel discovered that willpower has both immediate and future benefits. In this experiment, using marshmallows as bait, he tested children's ability to withstand temptation and exert self-control. Amazingly, he was able to predict the children's long-term success based on their level of willpower – for the following few decades!

In other words, better self-control leads to better outcomes in many areas of life, including financial status and physical health. No doubt, willpower is an important asset!

With that in mind, let's consider how to maintain the willpower you've developed throughout this course, which will no doubt improve your future.

One helpful technique is to look back and actively notice all the victories that you've had as you've practiced this course. **Remembering success is a great way to stay positive about what you've accomplished and keep it up, too.**

As you review your progress, you'll be reminded of what worked for you. Think about situations where you demonstrated perseverance, resisted temptation, or overcame laziness. Did you ever say to yourself, 'Wow, that took a lot of self-discipline!'? These are the actions that you want to keep repeating, as repetition builds habit – and your willpower muscle.

(Check out our Habit Workshop course  to learn how to maintain desired behaviors.)

You might also remember what didn't work, and where you felt willpower-challenged. In the book *Self-Discipline*, Dominic Mann reframes obstacles as opportunities for growth.
That's because you can learn from setbacks, too – like what mistakes not to repeat, where to be open to creative solutions, and how to persevere after the fact. When you're in a willpower mindset, you won't want to let failure stop you. Instead, you'll use it to your advantage.

Hopefully, what we've done here together during Willpower 101 will just be the beginning of your willpower journey. There's more work ahead and thankfully, together, we've set up the proper groundwork to keep you going.

DRIVING THE MESSAGE HOME

As we approach the end of Willpower 101 we will look back at the journey we have gone through together. Looking back will not only refresh our memory, but hopefully give us new insights into the journey we have gone through together.

There is no better way to end this journey than with Behavioral economist Dan Ariely talking about self-control. Not only will he help us recap what we have learned together, but he'll do it with a little twist of humor.

Let's get started.

Watch 'Self control' presented by Dan Ariely at TEDxDuke on YouTube.

You've been invited by Oprah to share your wisdom about willpower on national TV! Write some notes in advance of your appearance about how Willpower 101 helped you. Think about what worked best for you throughout the duration of the Willpower 101 course. You can include a particular "win" you had, an obstacle you overcame, and general encouragements for working on willpower.

TIPS

Tip 1: Remember, this is Oprah, so no false modesty! You can be as proud of yourself as you want—that's why people are tuning in!

Tip 2: Refer back to these notes in your journal whenever you need a motivational boost.

Extroverts are better at thinking positively

You may feel like you're at an advantage in life if you're an extrovert. And you wouldn't be wrong. Extroverts really have wonderful skills – but does that make them better at positive thinking?

For:

1. I'm not an extrovert myself, but I see how outgoing they are, and they seem to have a way of talking that makes other people around them feel good.
2. When you're an extrovert, you want to connect to the people around you. You've got to practice good social skills to have good relationships, and a piece of that is thinking positively.

Add you own argument:

3. ____

Against:

1. Positive thinking is a trait or a habit. Anyone can have it, whether introverted or extroverted.
2. In fact, I would say the opposite. Introverts, who spend more time thinking, are more likely to have a positive point of view.
3. Just because you're outgoing and gregarious doesn't mean you're not negative or grouchy. There is zero correlation.

Add you own argument:

4. ____

7 Positive thinking tips for introverts

You sometimes wonder why you seem so different from those 'other' folks – you know, the extroverted ones… Remember, being an introvert is more common and wonderful than you might think, and here's how to keep your thinking positive.
(Plus: Check out our Own your Introversion course.)

1. Stop comparing yourself to extroverts, because that's like comparing apples and pen-pineapple-apple-pens. Instead, remind yourself what you like most about being an introvert.
2. Measure your successes with your own personal yardstick. In other words, if it was difficult for you and you did it, that's great, and you deserve to give yourself credit!
3. Focus on the positive in your life. Anything can be looked at with a positive angle if you try.
4. Use humor to keep things light and right, even if it's just in your own head. Share the joke, and you'll be spreading joy to others.

Add your items to the list:

5. ____

6. ____

7. ____

Can you have too much willpower?

You've been working really hard on upping your willpower – good on ya! But what now? Is there an end in sight or do you just keep on going *ad infinitum*?

For:

1. Any virtue can become a vice when taken too far.
2. Being unnecessarily rigid could lead to more extreme forms of psychological inflexibility.
3. As important as willpower is, sometimes other values and priorities trump it. Life is about having all the tools you need at your disposal and using them intelligently, as needed.

Add your own argument:

4. ____

Against:

1. It's never enough. We need all the willpower we can get to help us successfully resist temptations that face us wherever we go, wherever we look.
2. We need willpower to get moving and keep up with our grown-up lives and responsibilities. Some days it's dang hard to be an adult. Only willpower will get us through.
3. Sometimes you need to drawn on your willpower reserves – like when you encounter uber-challenges. In those times, it helps to actually *have* reserves to draw upon!

Add your own argument:

4. ____

How I know my willpower journey ain't over yet

You'll need willpower for your future, surely… But how do you know that you've still got more growing to do? What taught you that you aren't quite "there" yet? Spend five minutes writing about your willpower journey in your 'Willpower 101' journal.

Direct message us YOUR story @Buddy_N_Soul on Instagram and be anonymously featured for a chance to **win a Buddy&Soul three month free membership**.

Using your willpower muscles is quite a feat, generally speaking. But we all have that *one* (or two or three... Don't judge us!) Big-Bad, the monster it takes all of our willpower to overcome. What was your Willpower Big-Bad, and how did you overcome it? Share your struggle, tips, and successes with the community and help inspire others who may be dealing with similar baddies! Spend five minutes writing about your experience harnessing your in your 'Willpower 101' journal.

Direct message us YOUR story @Buddy_N_Soul on Instagram and be anonymously featured for a chance to **win a Buddy&Soul three month free membership**.

WHERE DO WE GO FROM HERE?

You've finished the Willpower 101 book, but you haven't finished the journey. It doesn't end, it just gets better. Revisit this book, carry its ideas with you. Check out BuddynSoul.com and the rest of our books for all we have to offer. Spread the word. And change your life for good.

Cultivating Authenticity

Being an authentic person means being true to yourself
and knowing *how* to be yourself. It means
making choices that leave you feeling empowered, moving
through the world with integrity. It's tough living life with
the feeling of, "I don't know who I am," and this course
will help you on the road to authenticity by delving into
what "being real" means to you, what masks you hide
behind and why, and how you can bring to the world all
the beauty and joy of who you are and who you want to
be.

Goals you can achieve by reading 'Cultivating Authenticity':

- Understand and accept all the parts of who you are, behind your armor.
- Gain tools to live with a greater sense of integrity, inner alignment, and balance.
- Bring to the forefront all the beauty and joy of who you truly are.

Declutter Your Mind

You want to feel empowered. You want to live with clarity and peace of mind. But sometimes you find you might be weighed down by mental clutter, negative thoughts, and a general sense of being reoccupied and feeling overwhelmed. You can't move forward without first doing some emotional digging. This course will help you tackle some of your negative thoughts, harmful biases, unpleasant emotions, and stinging memories that are making you wonder why you can't focus, while hogging prime real estate in your mind. So, lighten your load and make space for a mind free of mental clutter, anxiety, stress, or feeling overwhelmed with life. Clutter free mind, here we come!

Goals you can achieve by reading 'Declutter Your Mind':

- Identify what's cluttering your mind, and why.
- Let go of negative thoughts, emotions, memories, and even people.
- Approach life with increased clarity, serenity, inner peace, and peace of mind.

Stress Management

Feeling stressed, anxious and overwhelmed? Now's the time to take a deep breath and ask yourself how your stress levels are impacting your life and health. While you might not be able to change your circumstances, this course will help you identify your recurrent stressors and teach you to avoid, work around, or effectively cope with them. The road to calm starts here.

Goals you can achieve by reading 'Stress Management':

- Identify and understand the stressors in your life.
- Learn simple and practical techniques for stress management.
- Create a lasting, less-stressful environment for yourself.

WANT TO LEARN MORE? CHECK THESE OUT!

BOOKS

Willpower: Rediscovering the Greatest Human Strength by Roy F. Baumeister and John Tierney

In this NY Times bestseller, Roy Baumeister, the world's leading willpower researcher, and science writer John Tierney reveal the secret of willpower and how to master it.
In this book you will find all you need to know about willpower, and how you can enhance your willpower one step at a time.

The Willpower Instinct: How Self-Control Works, Why It Matters, and What You Can Do to Get More of It by Kelly McGonigal

Based on the course she developed at Stanford University, Kelly McGonigal offers practical and useful advice on how to promote self-control, which really is a sister to willpower. In this book, she explains what willpower is, how it works, and why it matters. She gives advice and exercises to help with different goals in life along the way.

A great starting point for anyone who wants to get to the root of their willpower!

GADGETS AND OTHER PRODUCTS

Jet Puffed Snowman Mallows

You know all about the classic Stanford marshmallow experiment and now you're ready to test the willpower of some of the children (or adults!) in your life. Teach others what willpower is really all about with this short, fun experiment, using these delicious French vanilla marshmallows.

Meditation cushion

Meditate more comfortably using this cushion. It helps with spine alignment & helps prevent stress on your body, allowing for longer meditation.

Some find meditating and deep relaxation to be great ways to recharge their willpower.

MOVIES

Bridget Jones' Diary (2001)

In this light comedy, watch the main character try to stick to a series of new resolutions: no more drinking or smoking, not being paranoid about her weight, developing poise, and avoiding any romantic attachments.

Does she have enough willpower to succeed? Or is she overusing that willpower muscle?

El Perque de tot Plegat (What's It All About) (2002)

In this Spanish film (with English subtitles), 15 different human traits are depicted in short episodes, with willpower and doubt as the focal elements affecting human behavior.

Watch for great new insights about what makes our struggles with willpower so complex.